Design & Concepts L.L.C
October Issue

House of:
Lisabeth Design
Magazine

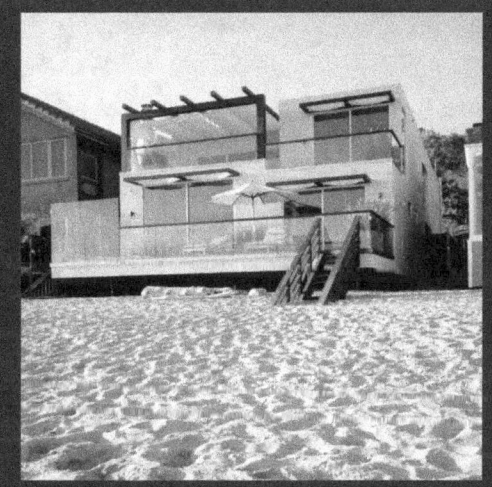

Today's Issue:

- *Doggy's world*
- *Fashion No's*
- *Design or Not*
- *Featured Business*

House of Lisabeth Design Magazine 2014

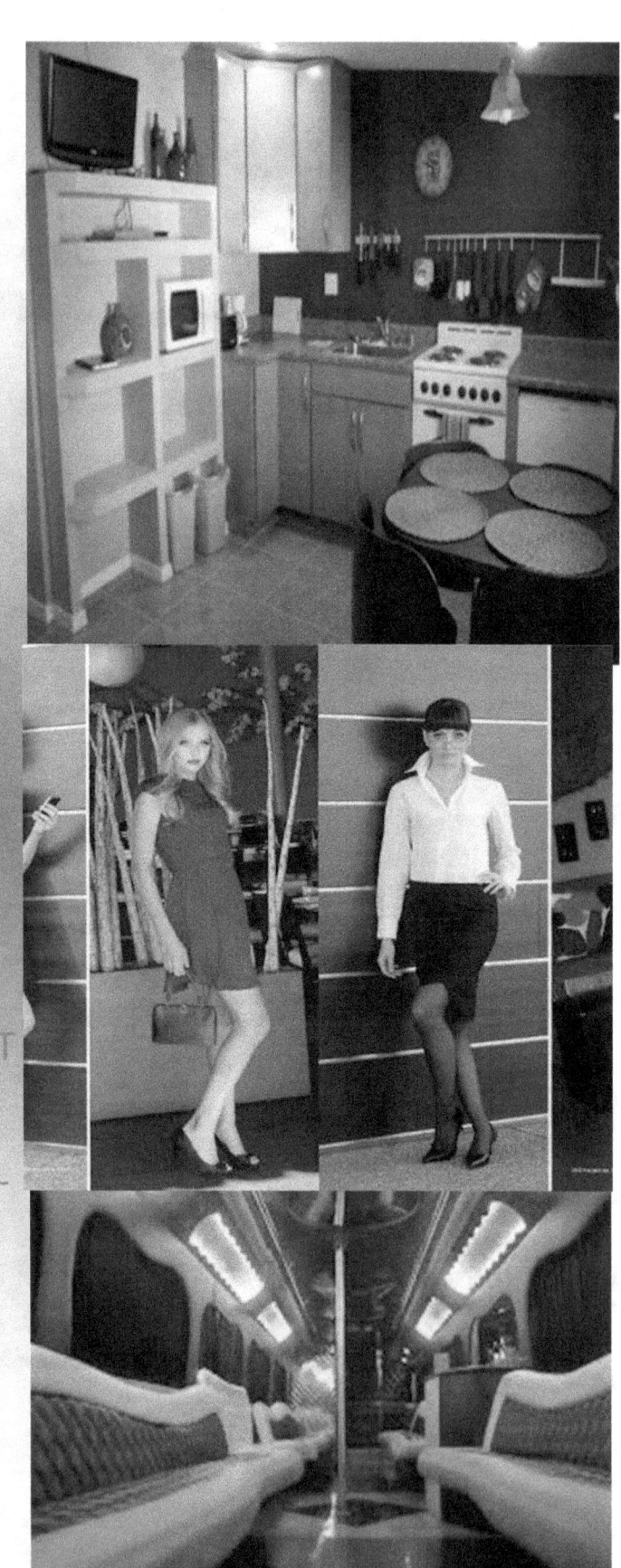

<u>Health and Trends: What we know and what you need to know…...</u>

<u>Oral Care, How clean are your teeth?</u>

When you're a busy active person sometimes its easy to forget to brush. We've all been a person of , ill just rinse with soap and water, or ill just buy some mint and suck really hard. Although you have a busy schedule that starts at 4 am or so you have to remember to take care of those things that shine the most.

Here is an overview of having healthy gums…..

Oral problems, including bad breath, dry mouth, canker or cold sores, TMD, tooth decay, or thrush are all treatable with proper dignosis and care. Its starts with the oral health, Having a good oral health plan is number one. First you want to understand your own oral health needs. Talk with your dentist, other oral health care specialist, or hygienist about any special conditions in your mouth and any ways in which your medical/health conditions affect your teeth or oral health. For example, cancer treatments, pregnancy, heart diseases, diabetes, dental appliances (dentures, braces) can all impact your oral health and may necessitate a change in the care of your mouth and/or teeth. Secondly you need to develop and follow a daily oral health routine.

Editors Feature

This means that you have to develop a daily routing that best fits your needs. If you have any special conditions such as diabetes or pregnancy then you have to develop your schedule for those needs. Its really basic elementary. Thirdly you need to use fluoride. It has been proven that children and adults who use fluoride at an early stage develop strong teeth. You also want to brush and floss daily. Using a floss can prevent cavity build up and other tooth related problems. Also you can have fun with floss such as flavored or the chewable. Anything to get you flossing. Lastly remember to eat a balanced healthy diet. Eat a variety of foods, but eat fewer foods that contain sugars and starches (for example, cookies, cakes, pies, candies, ice cream, dried fruits and raisins, soft drinks, potato chips). These foods produce the most acids in the mouth, which begin the decay process. If you do snack, brush teeth afterward or chew sugarless gum.

Notes and research
www.webmed.com

Are you grinding your teeth?

Teeth grinding happens from time to time. Now it doesn't cause harm but really if you do it enough it can get annoying.

Why Do People Grind Their Teeth?

Although teeth grinding can be caused by stress and anxiety it often occurs during sleep and is more likely caused by an abnormal bite or missing or crooked teeth. One thing is to see some one grinding there teeth with the chizzes coming off and you feel it crawling down your back and giving you the chills. Another is seeing that your best friend has some kind of anxiety problem and they are ruining there teeth because of it.

What Can I Do to Stop Grinding My Teeth?

Your dentist can fit you with a <u>mouth guard</u> to protect your teeth from grinding during sleep.

If stress is causing you to grind your teeth, ask your doctor or dentist about options to reduce your stress. Attending stress counseling, starting an exercise program, seeing a physical therapist, or obtaining a prescription for muscle relaxants are among some of the options that may be offered.

- Avoid or cut back on foods and drinks that contain <u>caffeine</u>, such as colas, chocolate, and coffee.

- Avoid alcohol. Grinding tends to intensify after alcohol consumption.
- Do not chew on pencils or pens or anything that is not food. Avoid chewing gum as it allows your jaw muscles to get more used to clenching and makes you more likely to grind your teeth.

Train yourself not to clench or grind your teeth. If you notice that you clench or grind during the day, position the tip of your <u>tongue</u>between your teeth. This practice trains your jaw muscles to relax.

Relax your jaw muscles at night by holding a warm washcloth against your cheek in front of your earlobe.

Opinions Section

My boyfriend has some personal problems and recently went to the doctor......

Me and my boyfriend have been going out for five years, and recently we ran into some medical issues. I had told him that I loved him and will support him in his decisions, but really I didn't want to tell him I didn't know what to do. He recently went to go see a doctor for some testosterone therapy. Its been a few weeks and things are fine do you think this was a good choice?

Recent studies have shown that testosterone therapy has a increased risk to heart related illness. For you to take the first step to getting your self checked is bravo to you. Here some more info about this.........

A 2014 study reported that testosterone therapy might increase the risk of a heart attack in men age 65 and older, as well as in younger men who have a history of heart disease. Also 2013 study found a higher frequency of death and heart problems in men who had coronary artery disease and received testosterone therapy. Also, a 2010 trial of testosterone in older men was stopped early because the men receiving testosterone therapy had a higher frequency of heart problems than did the men receiving the placebo. Keep in mind that testosterone therapy carries various other risks, including contributing to sleep apnea, stimulating noncancerous growth of the prostate, enlarging breasts, limiting sperm production, stimulating growth of existing prostate cancer and blood clots forming in the veins. If you wonder whether testosterone therapy might be right for you, talk with your doctor about the risks and benefits. If you are taking testosterone, make sure your doctor is monitoring your response to treatment with regular blood tests.

New Age Doctors : The new breed of medical warriors

According to the new age, new times and new ae we are open to ways of healing ourselfs. I agree vs pain is something elese. Lets lok at some facts....

Deepak Chopra (/ˈdiːpɑːk ˈtʃoʊprə/) (born October 22, 1947) is a controversial Indian-American author, New-Age guru, alternative-medicine advocate, public speaker and physician.[2][3] Through his several dozen books and videos, he has become one of the best-known and wealthiest figures in the holistic-health movement.[4]

Chopra obtained his medical degree in India before emigrating in 1970 to the United States, where he specialized in endocrinology and became Chief of Staff at the New England Memorial Hospital (NEMH). In the 1980s he began practicing transcendental meditation (TM) and in 1985 resigned his position at NEMH to establish the Maharishi Ayurveda Health Center. Chopra left the TM movement in 1994 and founded the Chopra Center for Wellbeing.[5]

Chopra states that, combining principles from Ayurveda (Hindu traditional medicine) and mainstream medicine, his approach to health incorporates ideas about the mind-body relationship, a belief in teleology in nature and a belief in the primacy of consciousness over matter – that "consciousness creates reality."[6] He claims that his practices can extend the human lifespan and treat chronic disease. This position is criticized by scientists, who say his treatments rely on the placebo effect; that he misuses terms and ideas from quantum physics (quantum mysticism); and that he provides people with false hope that may obscure the possibility of effective medical treatment.[7]

Festivals and Events

October 1

Chambers of Fear Haunted House and Bell Mar Bash
Surprise - Bell Mar Plaza
Chambers of Fear Haunted House and Bell Mar Bash – Bell Mar Plaza, annual haunted house which includes many featured events all month, nights filled with fund, food and fright, graveyard entertainment, 623-255-6896 or http://chambersoffear.com

October 2

20th Annual Schnepf Farms Pumpkin & Chili Party
Queen Creek - Schnepf Farms
20th Annual Schnepf Farms Pumpkin & Chili Party - Hillbilly Bob's pig races, spooky train rides, live entertainment, carousel, petting barn, 4-acre and Celebrity 10-acre maize, bon fires, pumpkin patch, hayride, Stuntmasters BMX show, Frisbee dog show, roller coaster and more, fireworks, $17 plus tax, Th & Su 10 am – 9 pm, Fr-Sa 10 am – 10 pm, 480-987-3100 or http://www.Schnepffarms.com

October4

Vintage Bisbee Wine Festival

Bisbee

Vintage Bisbee Wine Festival - sample more than 50 Old/New World wines, food by local restaurants live music, sponsored by the Bisbee Rotary Club, $45, 4-7 pm, 520-432-2071 or http://www.discoverbisbee.com or http://www.bisbeerotaryclub.org

October 4

Old Congress Days

Congress

Old Congress Days – parade, gymkhana, vendors, music, activities for children, BBQ, old fashioned gold panning, fine art show, beer garden, bake sale, raffle drawing, https://www.facebook.com/oldcongressdays

The World of Entertainment

TOP PICKS OF THIS MONTH.....

Four: A Divergent Collection
By: Veronica Roth

Two years before Beatrice Prior made her choice, the sixteen-year-old son of Abnegation's faction leader did the same. Tobias's transfer to Dauntless is a chance to begin again. Here, he will not be called the name his parents gave him. Here, he will not let fear turn him into a cowering child

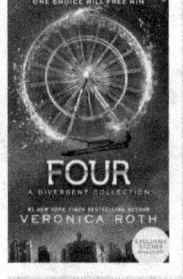

Heaven is for real: A little boys outstanding story of his trip to heaven and back
By: Todd Burpo Lynn Vincent (with)

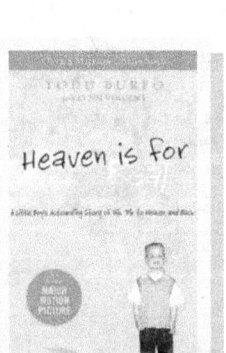

"A beautifully written glimpse into heaven that will encourage those who doubtand thrill those who believe."Ron Hall, coauthor of Same Kind of Different as Me"Do you remember the hospital, Colton?" Sonja said."Yes, mommy, I remember," he said. "That's where theangels sang to me."

Killing Patton: The Strange Death of World War II's Most Audacious General
By: Bill O'Reilly, Martin Dugard

Readers around the world have thrilled to Killing Lincoln, Killing Kennedy, and Killing Jesus—riveting works of nonfiction that journey into the heart of the most famous murders in history.

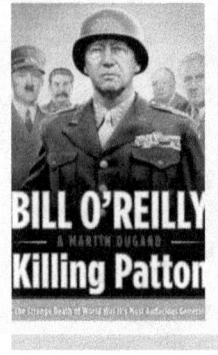

Dog Eat Dog World Presents:
Music Events, Concerts, Venue

U.S. Airways Center Presents

November 10
The black key with Jake Bug

November 29
Joan Sebation

201 E Jefferson St. Phoenix, AZ 85004 602-379-7878

Marquee Theatre Presents

**October 2
Bombay Bicycle Club**

**October 5
New Found Glory**

**October 6
Social Distortion**

1 E Main St. Mesa, AZ 85201 480-644-6501

Fashion No or not....
Brought to you by: Lisabeths Design

Kosher pants kosher everything

being kosher is like being one demoniation toward a color or fabric. It happens because we assume that this mean s fashionable or life but what we notice is it is our life. the every day we look we represent the life we believe.

 in things go together naturally, like peas and carrots. And certain things don't, like toothpaste and orange juice.

The Torah teaches about the power of combinations and warns against mixing the wrong things together. One of these is the prohibition against wearing a mixture of wool and linen in the same piece of clothing, as it is written, "You shall not wear combined fibers, wool and linen together" (Deut. 22:11).

In Hebrew, this forbidden mixture is called "shatnez" (pronounced shot-nezz).

Shatnez is an acronym for "combed, spun and woven," which describes the stages in processing fabric: combing the raw fiber, spinning fibers into a thread, and weaving the threads into cloth.

The mitzvah of shatnez still applies today. We observe the mitzvah by checking manufacturer labels on the clothes we buy, and by sending suspicious items (like wool suits and coats) to a "shatnez laboratory" for checking.

Clothes are a unique part of being human: only people wear clothes. Shatnez is a constant reminder that all our actions must be "kosher."

Interestingly, "holy garments" are exempt from the prohibition of shatnez. For example, the special garments worn by a Kohen while serving in the Holy Temple contained both wool and linen. Similarly, it is theoretically permitted to wear tzitzit that has shatnez (though there are technical factors which don't allow this today). The explanation may be that these garments are already inherently "kosher."

DESIGN SEO STYLE CREATE SEO LIFE

Creating user generating content for design and con-

cepts.......

User generating content or campaigns can be as easy as

123.......

Listen to the sounds of your fans....

refers to a variety of media available in a range of modern

communications technologies. UGC is often pro-duced

through even collaboration;[1] it is created by goal-

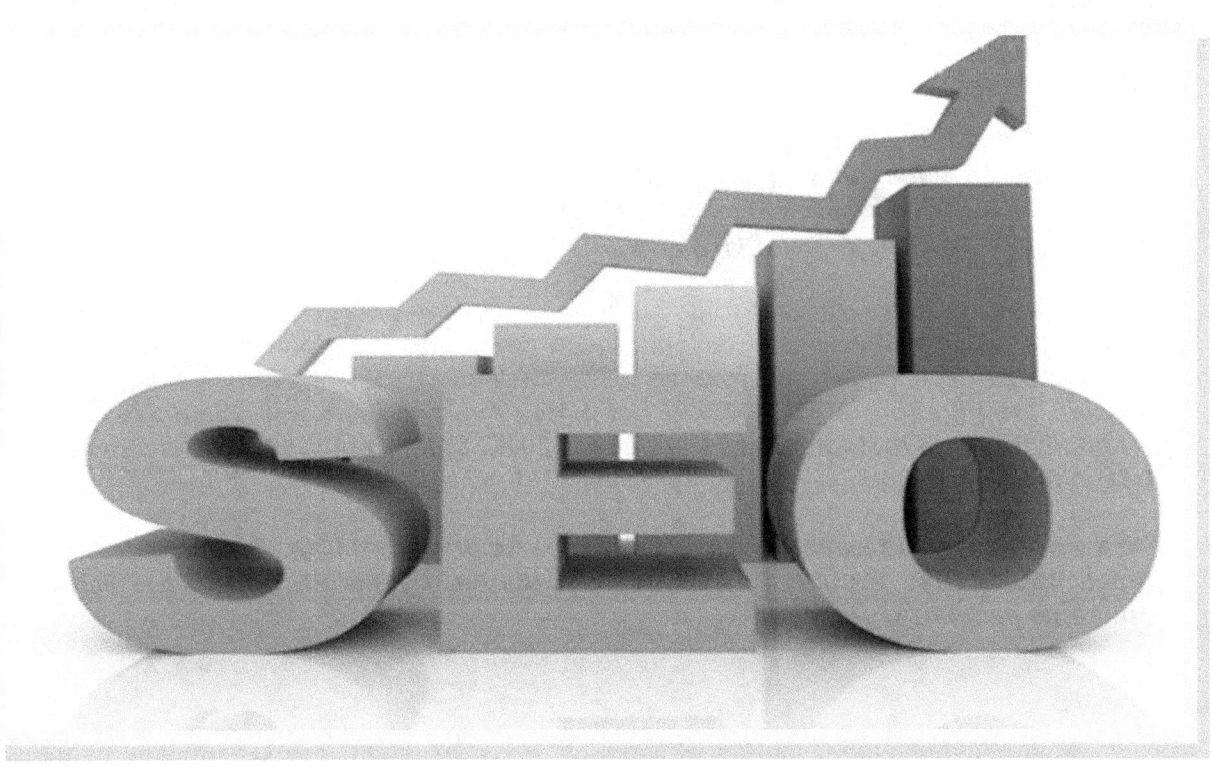

Panchos
3615 Highland AveManhattan Beach, CA 90266
Manhattan Beach

Ponchos
3615 Highland Ave Manhattan Beach, CA 90266
Manhattan Beach
310-545-6670

Welcome to Mexican with all the attraction. We love food that makes us go wow. Food that makes us break. An this is the place.

Poncho's is located at the intersection of Highland (Rosecrans) and PCH. It's an old looking rustic building, styled in the old Spanish architecture (complete with bricks poking out of the outside wall). I came here for brunch on a Sunday for a wedding rehearsal / planning meeting. How FUN!

First, know that this place is larger than it looks! There is a huge upstairs section which one side of the building is the bar and sports TV screens. The other side hosts about 15-20 table. Downstairs is just as huge! There must have been 20+ tables downstairs where the kitchen seemed to be located.

Because we came here during Sunday lunch (12:30), we were given a brunch menu. There were easily 15-20 different selections on the menu - ranging from eggs / molests, mole chicken, fajitas, burritos, etc. This brunch menu was a bit on the expensive side, ranging from $18.50 - $23.00 per plate. Average price was about $21. I personally thought that the prices were about 20% higher than most Mexican restaurants in the South Bay.

When we were seated, each person was given a fresh dish of fruit. Strawberries, grapes, apples were all super fresh. They also served a generous portion of fresh corn chips and salsa. Delicious!

Our waiter was Ramon. His badge states he has worked there for 37 years, and he has obviously spent this time perfecting the art of waiting a table because he didn't miss a beat during our time there.

Great service is awesome, but without some good food to go with it then it's not really worth having. Thankfully we weren't let down here. Before we had even ordered we were brought several plates of chips along with some really tasty salsa, spiced to perfection.

We ordered and our food arrived in good time, the portions were huge. The real blow me away moment came when I sampled a little bit of the guacamole. I don't know why I did it, I don't even like guacamole, but this was different. It tasted so creamy and light, if I'd had my eyes closed I would have sworn I was eating something else and before I knew it I just kept coming back for more. Turns out I do like guacamole after all, I've just only ever had bad guacamole before!

Thanks to our friends at Yelp.com

French-speaking painters continued the Mannerist conventions even later than did those at Haarlem, and at Nancy (capital of the independent duchy of Lorraine before 1633 and again from 1697 to 1766) a group of artists around Jacques Bellange and Jacques Callot was responsible for the last great flowering of the Mannerist style in Europe. By comparison, painting in Paris during the first decades of the 17th century was relatively insignificant, with the exception of that of Claude Vignon, who exchanged his Mannerist training for a style based on Elsheimer and to a lesser extent Lastman, and who in the 1620s revealed a remarkable knowledge of the earliest paintings of Rembrandt. The return of Simon Vouet to Paris, however, marked the arrival of the Baroque in France. The earliest paintings from his stay in Rome are strikingly vigorous essays in the Caravaggesque style, but by 1620 he was painting in an eclectic, classicizing style based on the early Baroque painters active there, including Giovanni Lanfranco and Guido Reni. This style he brought back to France, enjoying until his death an immense success in Paris as a decorator and painter of large-scale altarpieces; even the return of Nicolas Poussin failed to shake his position. Poussin's activity in Paris is of relatively little importance compared with the remainder of his career in Rome, but the large number of works commissioned by French patrons then and subsequently was an important factor in the formation of the French predilection for classicism. Another Frenchman, Claude Lorrain in Rome, had his sources in the romantic landscapes of the late Mannerists. By 1640 he established an international reputation. Both Poussin and Claude had been formed in Rome, but they remained typically French with a spiritual seriousness subjugated entirely to the laws of reason.

Trendy News What You Want To Know

John Abraham

(born May 6, 1978) is an American football outside linebacker of the National Football League (NFL). He is currently on leave from the Arizona Cardinals. He played college football for the University of South Carolina. Abraham was drafted by the New York Jets in the first round of the 2000 NFL Draft, and has also played for the Atlanta Falcons of the NFL.

Abraham's Week 1 concussion proved to be too much to overcome for the 36-year-old. After suffering the injury, Abraham went home to contemplate his future. He returned to the team this week, but couldn't pass the concussion protocol. The NFL's active sack leader with 133.5 of them, Abraham's career may be over

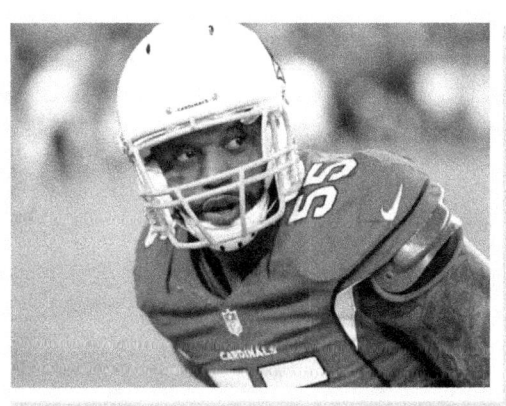
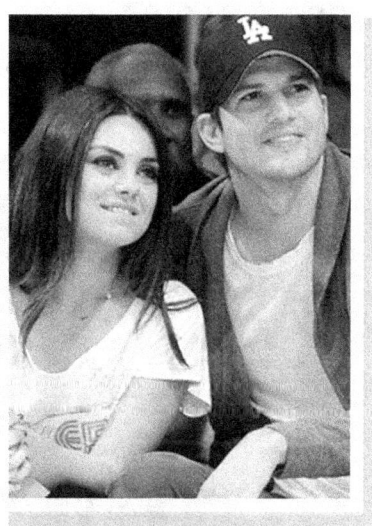

Soon after, Kunis told Ellen DeGeneres that she was planning on an epidural-free birth. "The hospital that I'm going to be laboring in does a midwife, you know, doula type of thing," she said.
"I'm going to do it as all natural as I possibly can unless there's an emergency or something that should go wrong. I did this to myself, I might as well just do it right. I wanted this!"
The former That '70s Show costars, who were first rumored to be dating in April 2012, have been happily preparing for their baby girl's arrival, with Kunis attending prenatal Pilates and yoga throughout her pregnancy and Kutcher doting on her.

New Technology For The Modern Geek

Funny C shape Magnetic

This high tech gadget also comes with a LED light feature that makes it look very cool when turned on in the dark
It is operated by an electronically controlled magnetic system.
The magnetic above the gadget contains an electro magnet and a magnetic field sensor
The base contains a micro-process

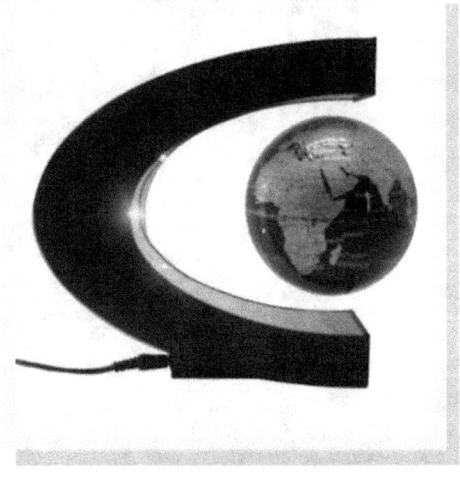

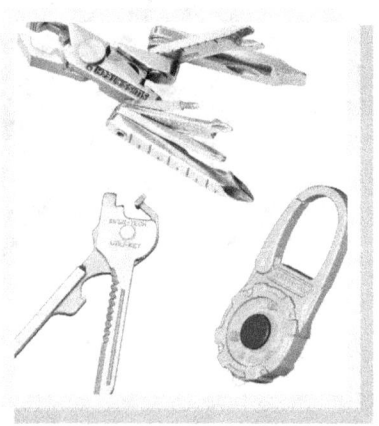

Swiss+Tech ST20027 Multi-Tool and LED Gift Box Set - 3 Piece
Gift for the tools and gadgets lover
With the utili-key, you can open bottles, packages, letters, and most screws
The 19-in-1 multi-tool includes multiple screwdrivers, pliers, bottle opener, wire cutter and stripper, wire crimper, hand drill, file, 2 rulers (millimeter and inch) and 2 ruler extensions (millimeter and inch)
Carabiner micro-light is a bright white LED flashlight with solid cast aluminum body for rugged durabilit

New Technology Vs. The other guys

Anthroposophy, a philosophy founded by Rudolf Steiner, postulates the existence of an objective, intellectually comprehensible spiritual world accessible to direct experience through inner development. More specifically, it aims to develop faculties of perceptive imagination, inspiration and intuition through the cultivation of a form of thinking independent of sensory experience,[1][2] and to present the results thus derived in a manner subject to rational verification. With a belief in a spiritual world, anthroposophy aims to attain the precision and clarity attained by the natural sciences in their investigations of the physical world.[1]

Anthroposophical ideas have been applied practically in many areas including Steiner/Waldorf education, special education (most prominently through the Camphill Movement), biodynamic agriculture, medicine, ethical banking, organizational development, and the arts. [1][3][4][5][6] The Anthroposophical Society has its international center at the Goetheanum in Dornach, Switzerland.

The early work of the founder of anthroposophy, Rudolf Steiner, culminated in his Philosophy of Freedom (also translated as The Philosophy of Spiritual Activity and Intuitive Thinking as a Spiritual Path). Here, Steiner developed a concept of free will based on inner experiences, especially those that occur in the creative activity of independent thought.[1]

By the beginning of the twentieth century, Steiner's interests turned to explicitly spiritual areas of research. His work began to interest others interested in spiritual ideas; among these was the Theosophical Society. From 1900 on, thanks to the positive reception given to his ideas, Steiner focused increasingly on his work with the Theosophical Society becoming the secretary of its section in Germany in 1902. During the years of his leadership, membership increased dramatically, from a few individuals to sixty-nine Lodges.[7]

By 1907, a split between Steiner and the mainstream Theosophical Society had begun to become apparent. While the Society was oriented toward an Eastern and especially Indian approach, Steiner was

Enhancement

Human enhancement refers to any attempt to temporarily or permanently overcome the current limitations of the human body through natural or artificial means. The term is sometimes applied to the use of technological means to select or alter human characteristics and capacities, whether or not the alteration results in characteristics and capacities that lie beyond the existing human range. Here, the test is whether the technology

In scientific usage, a phenomenon is any event that is observable, however common it might be, even if it requires the use of instrumentation to observe, record, or compile data concerning it. For example, in physics, a phenomenon may be a feature of matter, energy

a perturbation. Another example of scientific phenomena can be found in the experience of phantom limb sensations. This occurrence, the sensation of feeling in amputated limbs, is reported by over 70% of amputees. Although the limb is no longer present, they report still experiencing sensations. This is an extraordinary event that defies typical logic and has been a source of much curiosity

In recent decades, a new possibility for LGBT parenting, same-sex procreation (where two women could have a daughter with equal genetic contributions from both women, or where two men could have

sperm or male eggs from the cells of adult women and men. With female sperm and male eggs, lesbian and gay couples wishing to become parents would not have to rely on a third party donor of sperm or egg.

Social apps and more
Find us !

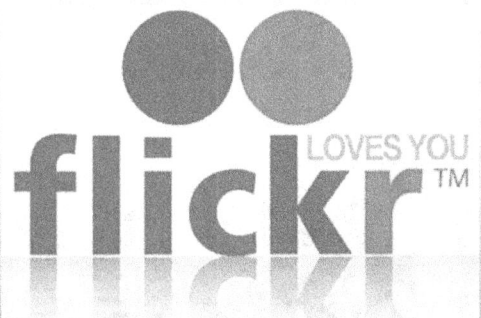

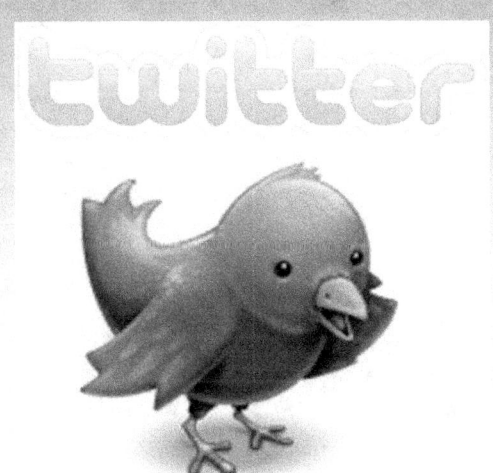

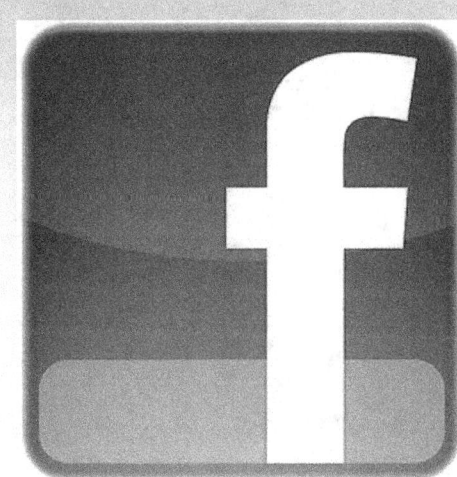

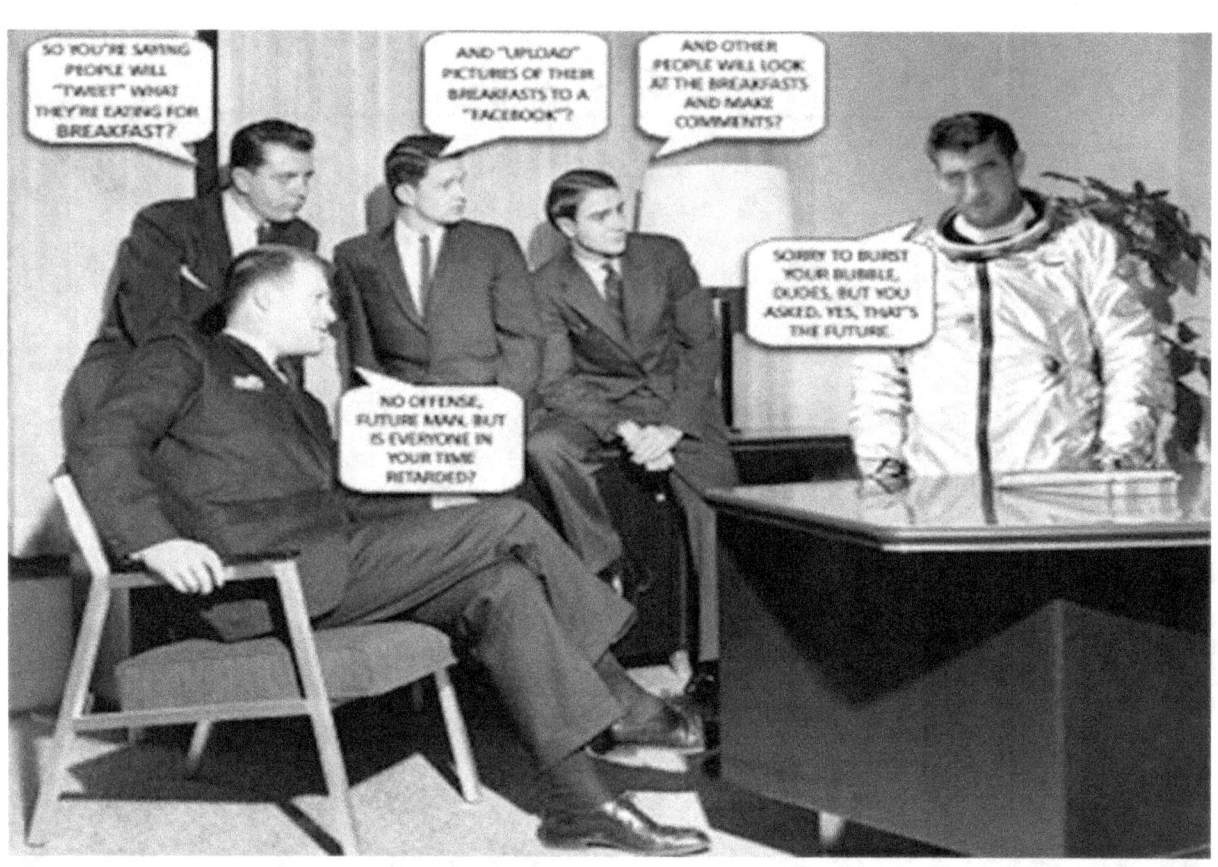

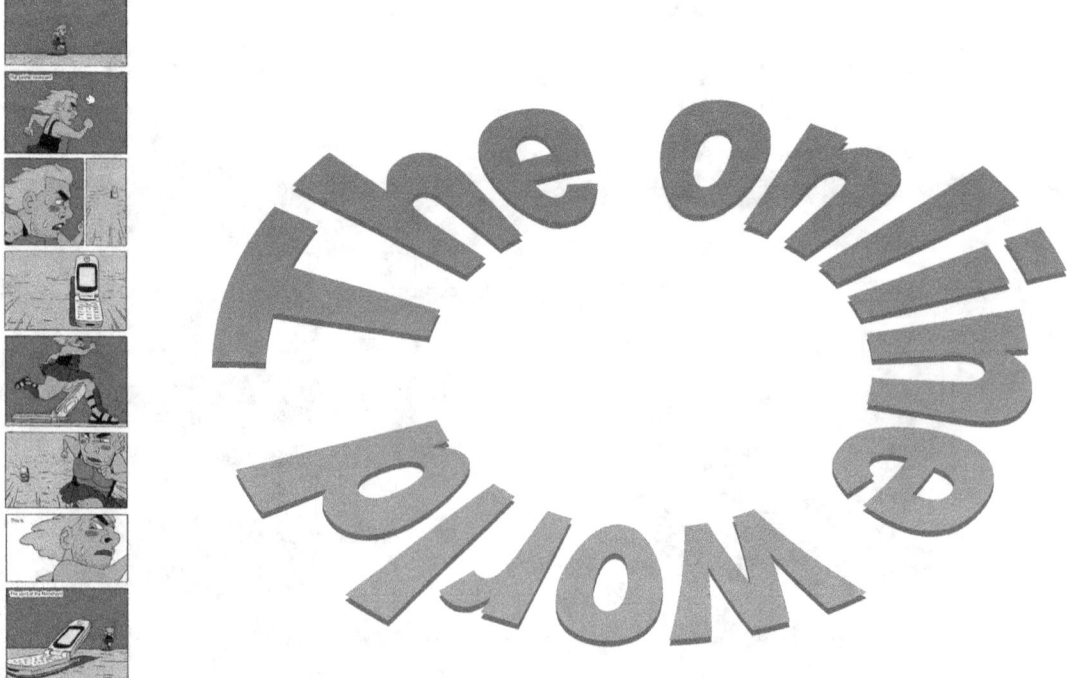

Business watch and what we need to know

North Korea digging tunnels in South

Gen. Hahn Sung-Chu never believed North Korea could dig a tunnel that reached Seoul -- until now.

Standing inside a basement of an apartment block in the heart of the capital, the former two-star general in the South Korean military says, "This is a kind of invasion, North Korean soldiers working underneath us."

Hahn says residents had complained of underground vibrations, but the subway does not run beneath them.

He says dowsers detected three tunnels, 13 to 16 feet (4 to 5 meters) wide at a depth of up to 39 feet (12 meters). His team drilled two bore holes to lower a camera, but before they could, they detected two underground explosions and their drill holes were blocked. Hahn is certain that North Korean soldiers were working beneath their feet, protecting the tunnel.

Secret Service Director Julia Pierson resigns

Julia Pierson, the first female director of the Secret Service, resigned Wednesday in the aftermath of a fence-jumper gaining access to the White House on September 19 and a subsequent congressional inquiry uncovering other security lapses.

Homeland Security Director Jeh Johnson announced the resignation in a statement. He also announced that the Department of Homeland Security would take over an internal inquiry of the Secret Service and that he would appoint of a new panel to review security at the White House.

Joseph Clancy, formerly a special agent in charge of the Presidential Protective Division of the Secret Service, was named interim director, Johnson said in his statement.

Hong Kong leader refuses to step down amid protests

A midnight deadline imposed by pro-democracy demonstrators calling for Hong Kong's top official to step down passed Friday, with Chief Executive C.Y. Leung vowing to stay and warning of "serious consequences" should protesters cross police lines.

Leung said Chief Secretary Carrie Lam, who is second in command, will meet with representatives of the Hong Kong Federation of Students to discuss "constitutional development matters." He urged protesters not to occupy the space outside official buildings, including government headquarters, police headquarters and Government House.

Survive The Realestate Market

The Mad Men Era: Cost of Living Then and Now
AMC's "Mad Men" has come to reflect styles and trends not only in fashion, but also in our home and office lives. Our infatuation with the award-winning television show has propelled us to delve deeper into the history of that era, particularly how the affordability of housing and the cost of living have changed over the course of the last half-century.
With the final season of Mad Men fast approaching, and a number of characters potentially moving to start a West Coast office for SC&P, we explored housing costs from the 1960s and how the costs of that era compare to today.

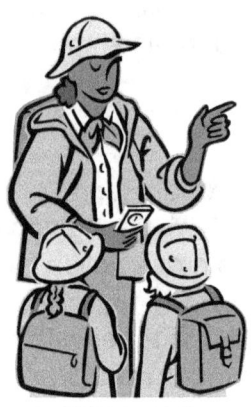

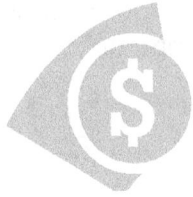

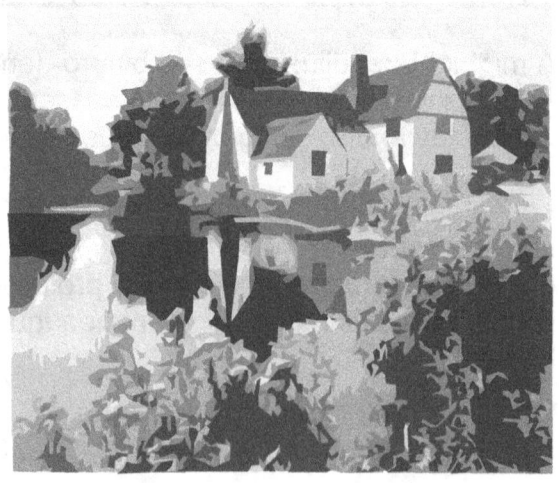

Politics and More

Accused White House fence jumper pleads not guilty

The man who allegedly jumped a White House fence last month and breached the mansion's doors pleaded not guilty Wednesday.

White House intrusion was 'unacceptable'

Secret Service: When to use deadly force?

A federal judge in the District of Columbia ordered additional mental testing on Omar Gonzalez, a 42-year-old Iraq war veteran, to determine whether he is competent to stand trial.

Secret Service director calls White House intrusion 'unacceptable'

The next court date is scheduled for October 21. Gonzalez will remain in custody.

Aaron Hernandez case: Who's who?

Former New England Patriot Aaron Hernandez is behind bars, accused of murdering three people.

Long before he made national headlines, he was a standout athlete in Bristol, Connecticut, who came from a family described as a local sports dynasty. Hernandez left high school halfway through his senior year in January 2007 to join the University of Florida Gators. He entered the NFL draft after his junior year and was selected by the Patriots in the fourth round.

By the end of the second season, he inked a five-year contract extension worth $40 million. But less than a year later, he was charged with first-degree murder in the death of Odin Lloyd. Two hours after his arrest on June 26, 2013, the Patriots dropped him from the team.

Hernandez has also been charged in the slayings of Daniel de Abreu and Safiro Furtado, and some of his closest associates are facing serious charges in connection with the alleged crimes.

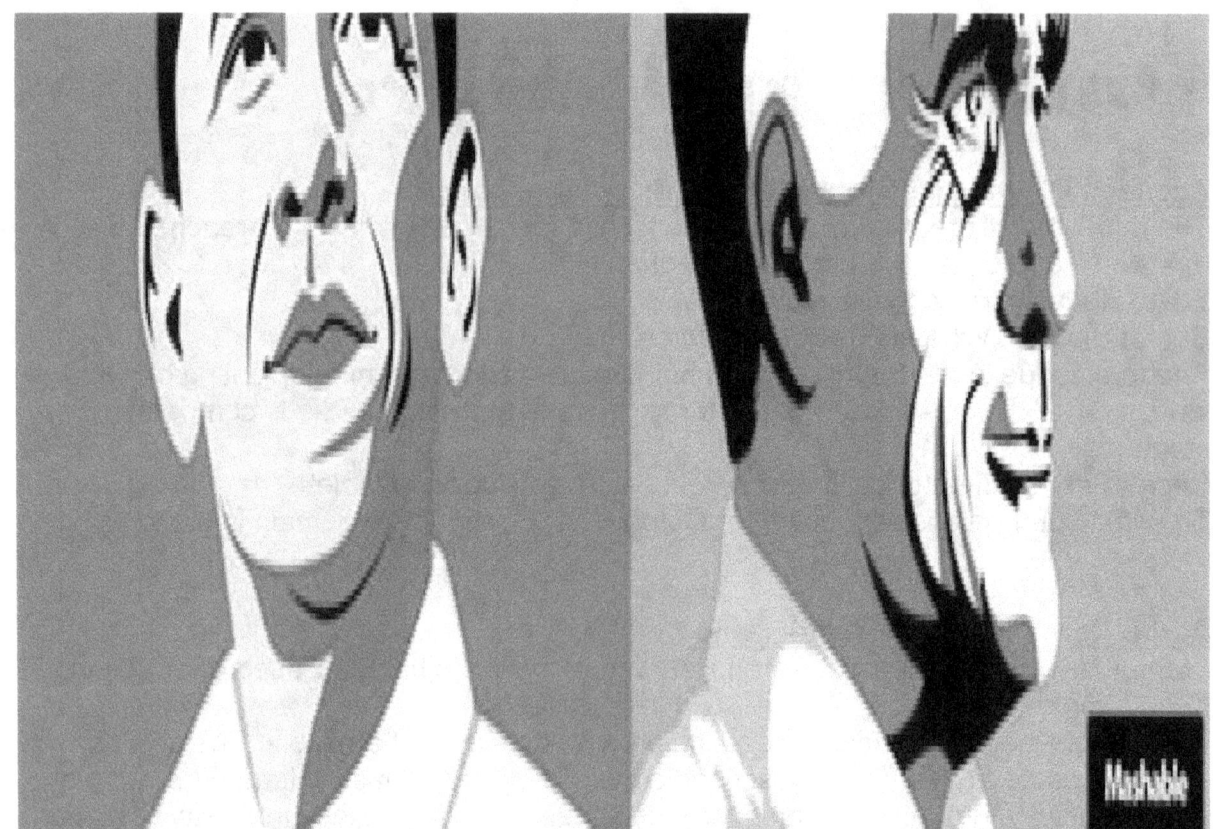

Politics Transformed

THE HIGH TECH BATTLE FOR YOUR VOTE

Politics: The who and what of Politics

Olympic swimmer Michael Phelps arrested on DUI charge

Legendary Olympic swimmer Michael Phelps, the most decorated Olympian of all time, was arrested early Tuesday in Maryland on a DUI charge, according to the Maryland Transportation Authority.

Phelps, known as the "Baltimore Bullet" and winner of 18 Olympic gold medals, was arrested at about 1:40 a.m. and charged with driving under the influence, excessive speed and crossing double lane lines within the Fort McHenry Tunnel on I-95 in Baltimore, the authority said in a statement. He was later released.

Phelps, who returned to competitive swimming in April, said on his official Twitter account that he understands the severity of his actions.

Like 'Ahab and the white whale,' man hunted missing daughter for 12 years

Greg Allen's obsession with finding his missing daughter began more than a decade ago, when the mother finally made good on a threat and fled with the daughter from Texas to Mexico, according to him and authorities.

Sabrina Allen was a month away from turning age 5, and the visit with her non-custodial mother, Dara Marie Llorens, was supposed to last only a weekend in April 2002, as part of a court agreement.

But that weekend visitation in Austin lasted 12 years and finally ended Tuesday, when Mexican and U.S. authorities said they found the girl and her mother living in seclusion in a small apartment in a town between Mexico City and Puebla. The mother will face charges in Travis County, Texas, said Dan Powers, an FBI assistant special agent in charge in San Antonio, Texas.

So much time has passed that Allen's daughter is all but grown, now 17 years old. Moreover, his daughter has been told over the years that her father was "a bad guy" and "a wife beater" -- all false accus

ations, Allen declared.

October 2014

Sunday	Monday	Tuesday	Wednesday	Thursday	Friday	Saturday
			1	2	3	4
5	6	7	8	9	10	11
12	13	14	15	16	17	18
19	20	21	22	23	24	25
26	27	28	29	30	31	

This month will be a great month!

October is Spooky

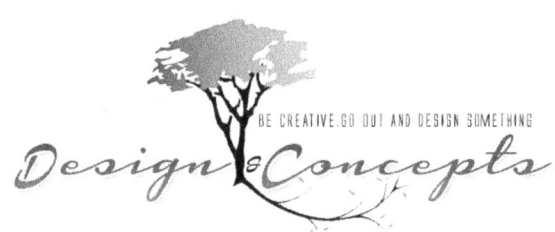

BE CREATIVE.GO OUT AND DESIGN SOMETHING

Design & Concepts

Join our mailing list
and get a free 1
month Subscription
to our magazine!

Owner

Design & Concepts L.L.C
Elizabeth Chavez
602-785-1108
www.designandconcepts.biz
www.lisabethdesignmagazine.com

Creativedesignconcepts@rocketmail.com

Place orders by email or contact

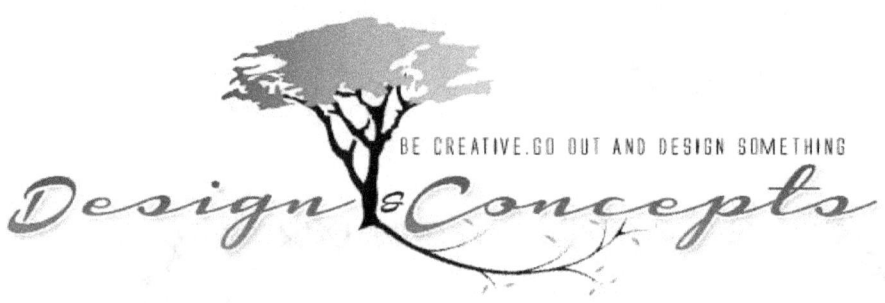

BE CREATIVE.GO OUT AND DESIGN SOMETHING

House of Lisabeths Design Magazine
We were started in 2013 as an independent magazine. Our focus is fashion, health and business. We pride ourselves in the design and diversity we offer.
Exclusivity
Our focus is fashion , health and business. Our fashion section includes tips and trends from all over! We also have a online blog that gets tons of clicks per day, check us out online at ......
Our business section is used for local or national business to place a Ad or listing of them selfs. We have total exclusivity In that they connect with not only our magazine but all of our networks simultaneously.
Our hope is to reach across the world along with Water 4 Kids International.
We plan to donate proceeds to this foundation. Our hope is to provide safe water for east Africa.
Check us out on line, Facebook, Twitter, Tumblr, Amazon, and our affiliates websites like Design & Concepts.

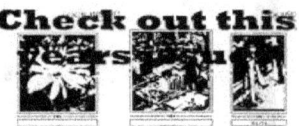

Get a 1 year subscription for $ 19.99——————————— ☐

Personal Information
Name:_____   Email _____

Address_____, Phone _____

City, State, Zip _____

Payment Enclosed——————————- ☐
Pay Later——————————————- ☐

Send To:

Design & Concepts

" Fill out above info and return to address given"
MIAMI
Liz Chavez
8369 NW 66 ST #3684
Miami, FL 33166

We also take check, cash and money orders.

Remember when you send for a subscription you get a free t-shirt that says "Lisabeth Design"

Thanks for supporting our fashion blog and Section!

Also with your subscription get a free Lisabeth Design T-Shirt

Available for Men and Women

Check out Design & Concepts Blog

DONT BUY MEAT
The worthy of the worth and the Elite of the Elite make a common general statement. " DONT BUY MEAT!" You may ask what dose this mean, no meat no nothing don't buy it if its not out there for a good reason or a beneficial reason don't buy it. I once took a seminar on how you can here 100 things at a time and not understand everything that you are listening to. For instance a commercial can advertise the same tactics, like hey we have this new and improve staple, but yet what is going to make you buy this new and improve staple in the first place. Putting away your needs and obvious i just so happened to lose my normal staple. You start to realize that you don't need the automatic closer, the quick throw back metal thing that snaps back faster then any other staple after you squeeze. You just need a super awesome staple. A staple the thing of necessity. So by saying this i again , build networks and offer professional opportunities. limitations of the human body through natural or artificial means. The term is sometimes applied to the use of technological means to select or alter human characteristics and capacities, whether or not the alteration results in characteristics and capacities that lie beyond the existing human

Join the Cause!
Check out the " Design for Sick Kids Campaign'

Our Mission
In the beginning we wanted a way to show our passion for design.
But this project is turning to be more then that. With so many sick
kids and so much that we can give we thought about giving the gift
of design.

What We Need & What You Get
Here is what we need
1000 cards , either designed by you or who ever
A contribution as well to our campaign

The Impact
With every card made we will donate a dollar and that card to a local
hospital of our choice. So think about all the kids you can help by
creating there Christmas card or birthday card and also the contri-
butions that come with it.
Remember every card made we donate $ 1.00 to the cause
Also share your design with the people and get your picture taken
with the kids

Other Ways You Can Help Check out our websites
www.designandconcepts.net for more updates on more causes!

http://www.indiegogo.com/projects/design-a-card-for-your-kids/

Join the Cause!

Check out the " House Of Lisabeth Design Magazine- We are Here"

Our Mission
House of Lisabeth Design magazine is a new trendy magazine for fashion, trends, and business networking.

Hi, my name is Elizabeth Chavez I am the owner of Design & Concepts and am the editor and creator of " House of Lisabeth Design Magazine"

We are reaching out to you for a launch of our new magazine. For us it's important to get contributors from people who have faith in this magazine and want to help us launch it.

What were looking for is anything from 1 dollar to 100 dollars...The more people we reach the faster we will get to our goal.

Remember be creative go out and design something!

Also be sure to check us out on Facebook, Twitter, Amazon, Tumblr and our affiliate blogs , Lisabeth blog, and Design and Concepts blog

Also with your subscription get a free Lisabeth Design T-Shirt

Available for Men and Women

Design & Concepts Services

www.Designandconcepts.biz
www.lisabethdesignmagazine.com

Design & Concepts is an online service provider for design and advertising. We specialize in brochures logos and business cards as well as t shirts and sickies. We also do local advertising with in the community. Our prices vary with design but...

Our packages start at $55.00 per package!
Package includes : 200 prints
Gloss or matt finish is $10.00 per set/ per 200

Our Packages also include our Marketing Services, and Discounts on our Advertising Specials in our magazine, House of Lisabeth Design Magazine!

Also with your subscription get a free Lisabeth Design T-Shirt

Available for Men and Women

Design & Concepts Services:

Create various ads and place it on all social networks, web pages and create you tube videos to sell, demonstrate and promote your product

Also place your ad on any media source that is available We can take your campaign and place it on any other media resources you have available not just create a web presence awareness but really hit the market.

.We use digital media like

Email marketing, social network campaigns, print distribution, custom Web Design and SEO

Funny Definition of the month

In the IT Industry, implementation refers to post-sales process of guiding a client from purchase to use of the software or hardware that was purchased. This includes requirements analysis, scope analysis, customizations, systems integrations, user policies, user training and delivery. These steps are often overseen by a project manager using project management methodologies. Software Implementations involve several professionals that are relatively new to the knowledge based economy such as business analysts, technical analysts, solutions architects, and project managers.

To implement a system successfully, a large number of inter-related tasks need to be carried out in an appropriate sequence. Utilising a well-proven implementation methodology and enlisting professional advice can help but often it is the number of tasks, poor planning and inadequate resourcing that causes problems with an implementation project, rather than any of the tasks being particularly difficult. Similarly with the cultural issues it is often the lack of adequate consultation and two-way communication that inhibits achievement of the desired results.

Looking for classifieds, if interested submit your business and information and well help you out!

Liz:
creativedesignconcepts@rocketmail.com

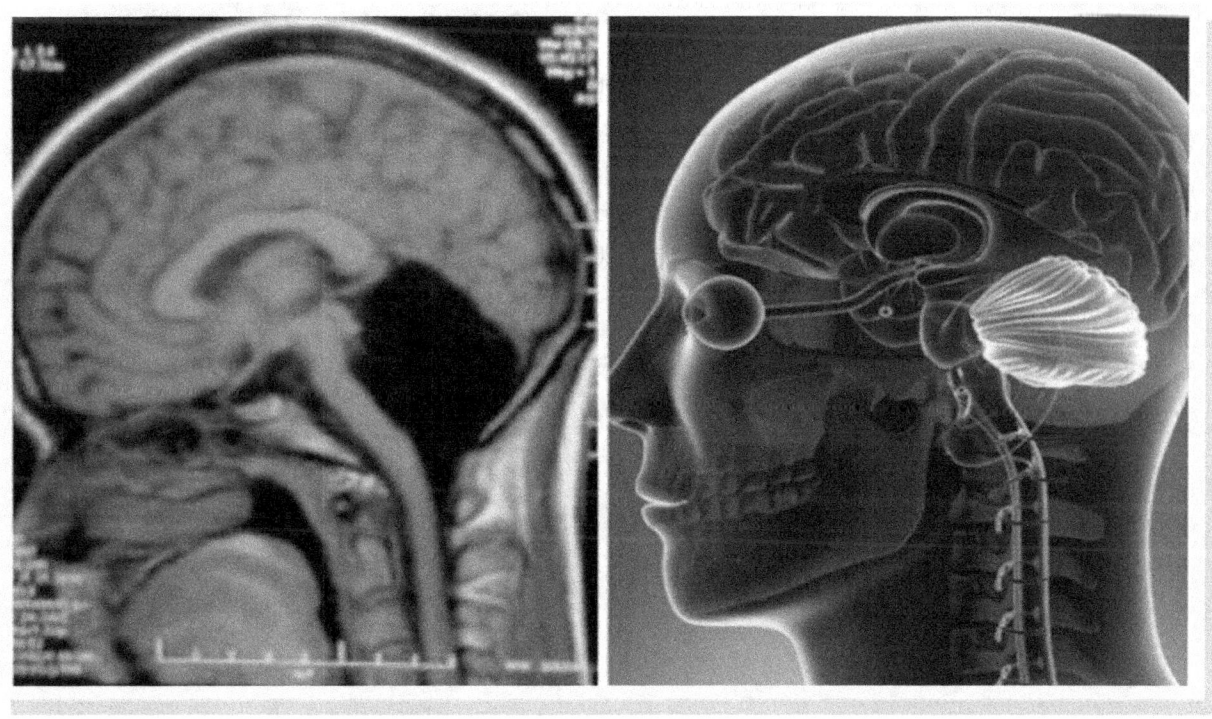

Meet The Editor And Owner.....

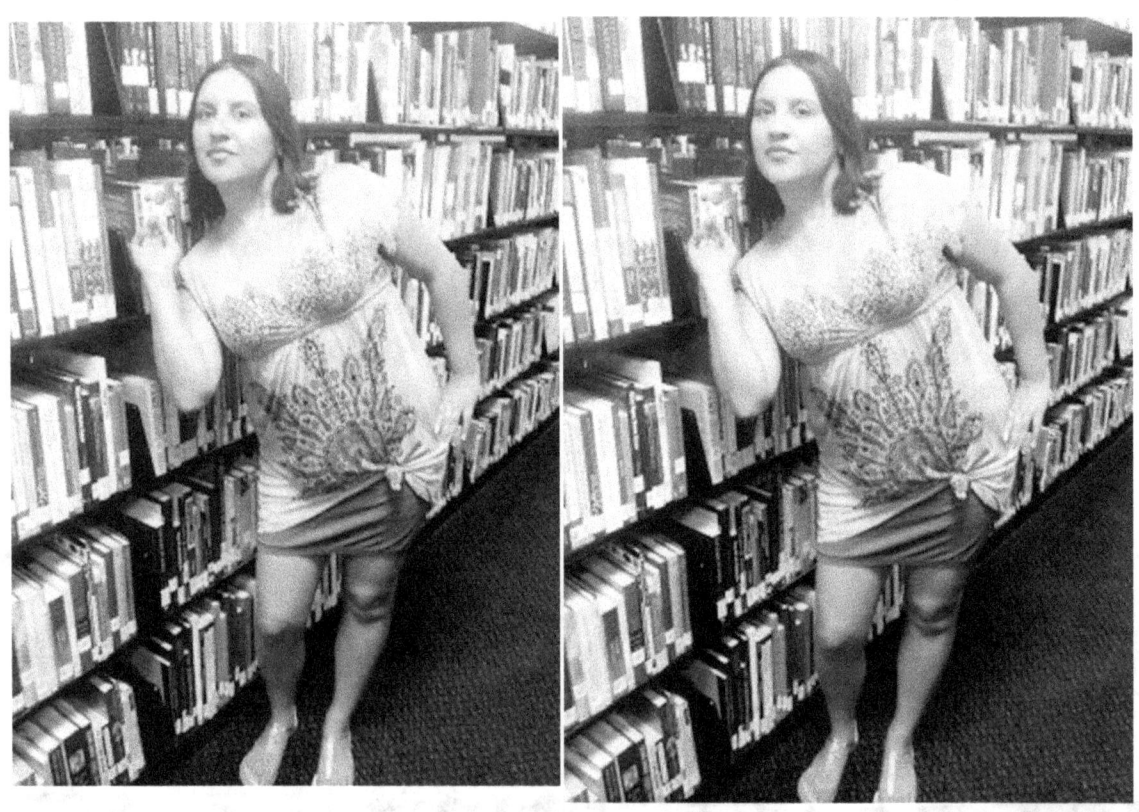

Elizabeth Chavez 27,,, Currently the owner of Design & Concepts LLC , and Editor of House of Lisabeth Design Magazine. As an entrepreneur in her own field she manages both her business and love of de-signing in her everyday life. She works hard by involving all things that she can in many projects that she is involved with. One of her favorite is the Design For Kids Campaign, for her this is not only about kids but about love of the community.

How to customize White Bowls

<u>Materials Needed:</u>
mixing bowls (such as nesting mixing bowls, crateandbarrel.com)
multi-surface satin acrylic paint (FolkArt lime green, ink spot, and daffodil yellow, plaidonline.com)
Chevron FrogTape Shape Tape (amazon.com)
letter stickers (Remarks Shortcake-Black stickers, americancrafts.com)
paint pens (Pebeo pen in scarlet red, emerald, agate orange, and bengal pink, markersupply.com)

<u>For Zigzags</u>

Starting at the top, apply strips of chevron tape around the bowl, spacing them 1.5 inches apart. (The tape won't wrap smoothly around the bottom part of the bowl, so cut it into smaller pieces and match them up to create a continuous zigzag.) Color in the spaces between the tape with porcelain paint, then peel off the tape. Follow the instructions on the paint's packaging for setting the color.

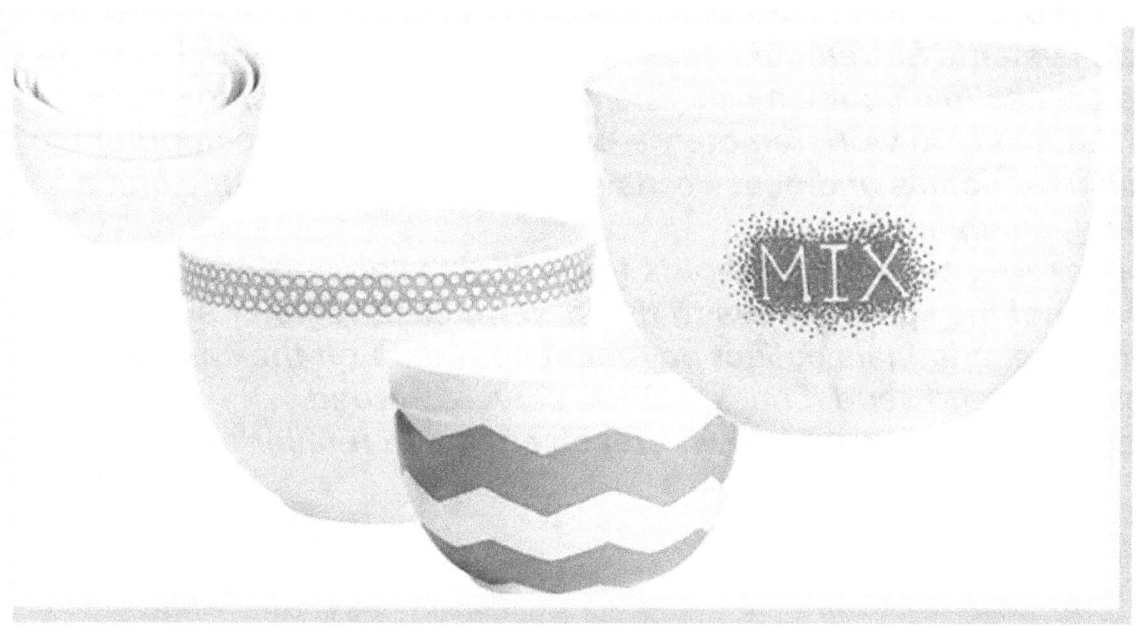

U.S. Finds 'Backoff' Hacker Tool Is Widespread
More than 1,000 American businesses have been affected by the cyberattack that hit the in-store cash register systems at Target, Supervalu and most recently UPS Stores, the Department of Homeland Security said in an advisory released on Friday.
The attacks were much more pervasive than previously reported, the advisory said, and hackers were pilfering the data of millions of payment cards from American consumers without companies knowing about it. The breadth of the breaches, once considered limited to a handful of businesses, underscored the vulnerability of payment systems widely used by retail stores across the country.
On July 31, Homeland Security, along with the Secret Service, the National Cy-bersecurity and Communications Integration Center and their partners in the se-curity industry, warned companies to check their in-store cash register systems for a malware package that security experts called Backoff after a word that ap-peared in its code. Until that point, Backoff malware and variations of it were un-detectable by antivirus products.
Some of those clients, like UPS and Supervalu, have stepped forward, but most have not.
In all, the Secret Service estimated that more than 1,000 American businesses had been affected.
According to the Secret Service, criminals are actively scanning corporate systems for remote access opportunities — a vendor with re-mote access to a company's systems, for example, or employees with the ability to work remotely — and then deploying computers to guess user names and passwords at high speeds until they find a working combination.
The hackers use those footholds to crawl through corporate net-works until they gain access to the in-store cash register systems. From there, criminals collect pay-ment card data off the cash regis-ter systems and send it back to their servers abroad.
Last year, in the largest known breach against a retailer's payment

Since then, seven companies that sell and manage in-store cash register systems have confirmed to government officials that they each had multiple clients affect-ed, the government said Friday. Some of those clients, like UPS and Supervalu, have stepped forward, but most have not.

In all, the Secret Service estimated that more than 1,000 American businesses had been affected.

According to the Secret Service, criminals are actively scanning corporate systems for remote access opportunities — a vendor with remote access to a company's systems, for example, or employees with the ability to work remotely — and then deploying computers to guess user names and passwords at high speeds until they find a working combination.

The hackers use those footholds to crawl through corporate networks until they gain access to the in-store cash register systems. From there, criminals collect pay-ment card data off the cash register systems and send it back to their servers abroad.

Last year, in the largest known breach against a retailer's payment

system, hackers invaded Target for weeks without being detected. The hackers' malware stole cus-tomers' data directly off the magnetic stripes of credit and debit cards used by tens of millions of shoppers. Gregg Steinhafel, Target's chief executive, and Beth M. Jacob, the company's chief information officer, stepped down from their posi-tions, largely because of the breach.

The Target breach exposed problems with the magnetic stripes on credit cards. Since then, banks and companies have taken a renewed interest in a chip-based smart card standard known as E.M.V., short for Europay-MasterCard-Visa, the technology's first backers. Credit card companies have set an October 2015 dead-line for American retailers to upgrade their payment systems.

"The weakness is the magnetic stripe," said Avivah Litan, a security analyst for Gartner Research. "I can buy a mag stripe reader on eBay and easily read all the data from your credit card. It's an antiquated technology from the '60s."

E.M.V. makes counterfeiting far more difficult than magnetic stripe cards, but ana-lysts say they believe that most retailers will not meet

the October 2015 deadline because of the cost to upgrade their terminals — from $500 to $1,000 per termi-nal, according to Javelin Strategy & Research. With cash register malware rampant, however, they may have no choice.

Millions of American consumers' payment card details are being sold on the black market, many of them taken from American companies that do not know their systems have been breached.

Unless companies search for Backoff on their systems, it can be difficult to identi-fy. The Homeland Security report released on Friday recommends that compa-nies contact their service providers, antivirus vendors and cash register system ven-dors to assess whether they have been compromised or are vulnerable to attack.